Secured and Fortified:
A Prayer Warrior's Guide to Victory

By

Dr. Ceretta A. Smith

Forward

With all that is going on in the natural and the spiritual realm, God has strategically placed intercessors to boldly come to his throne of grace. They must have faith to speak to mountains and cause winds and waves to obey them. They come in humility before God on behalf of those who for whatever reason are unable to come before God for themselves. An intercessor is not just one that prays but one that has been called by God to travail just like a mother agonizes in labor to bring forth her child. They are a threat to the devil because he realizes that they are armed and dangerous.

I pray that those that are reading this book and who are mandated to intercede, will continue to bombard heaven on behalf of those that are lost, those that are in need of a Savior, and those who are perplexed by the tricks and snares of the enemy. We need intercessors to boldly go where many have desired to go but could not. They need to go to the 'heavenlies' and cause a supernatural shift in the atmosphere that would move the hand of God. I encourage you; in fact, I summon you to buy this book and learn the elements of intercession that will catapult you to the next level of intercession so that when you are called for duty, you will be able to answer like a good soldier and go where others desire to go but do not know how. This book will definitely take you there.

This book has been birthed out of many long hours of intercession, trials and tribulations and Dr. Smith has applied the same principles outlined in this book to her life and has come out victorious countless times.

She has had to defend the visions that God has given her by securing and fortifying her position. After serving her country as an enlisted U.S. soldier and in God's army as a mouth piece for God, Dr. Smith is knowledgeable in the natural army as well as in the spiritual army. As she sounds the alarm for intercessors to mount up and defend the position of the local church by securing and fortifying it, hear the call and respond with a "Yes Lord."

–In His Purpose
Prophetess Enda Gibson
Waco, Texas

Dedication

I would like to dedicate this book to my grandmothers (Bernice Brodie and Alberta Scales), my aunts (Aunt Mary Lee, Aunt Jen Jen and Aunt Ora), the ladies of the Prayer Band and the Mothers of my home church and community (Mother Ida Haire, Miss Elaine, Miss Haire, Miss Lillie Mae and Mother Alma Brown). I grew up watching these women pray and wail before the Lord.

Truly they were skillful wailing women and now, as I reflect back on those times as a little girl hanging to their skirt tails, I realize even then that God was teaching me how to pray and touch heaven. Some of them have gone on to be with the Lord (Bernice Brodie, Mother Ida Haire, Miss Lillie Mae and Mother Alma Brown), but I am so humbled and honored to be a vessel to carry on their legacy.

Secured and Fortified:
A Prayer Warrior's Guide to Victory

Unless otherwise indicated, all scriptures are quoted from the King James, New International and New Living Translation Versions of the Bible.

Published by: **To His Glory Publishing Company, Inc.**
463 Dogwood Drive, NW
Lilburn, GA 30047
(770) 458-7947
www.tohisglorypublishing.com

This Book is available at:
Amazon.com, BarnesandNoble.com, Booksamillion.com, UK, Canada, Australia, etc.

Also, see the Order Form at the back of this book or call/email below to order this book.

Email: tohisglorypublishing@yahoo.com
(770) 458-7947
www.tohisglorypublishing.com

ISBN: 978-0-9854992-3-5

Table of Contents

Introduction

I have always been a person of prayer and let me also add that I am a person that wars in prayer. Being in the military and being a military spouse has afforded me the opportunity to travel and to be a part of many ministries over the years. It never failed that no matter what ministry I ended up in, I always found my way to the prayer group or was always invited to join the prayer group. During these times, I did not really have a lot of knowledge or understanding of intercession or warfare; or should I say any book knowledge. Therefore, all of my training and teaching was truly by the Holy Spirit.

As I began to come in contact with seasoned intercessors and prayer warriors and as they began to point me in the right direction, I began to read and study prayer and intercession. As a result, I began to get an understanding as to what I had been doing all those years. Not that I had arrived, but more than anything, this understanding let me know that I was right where God wanted me to be and that although I did not know it, I had been tapping into something very vital to the body of Christ. But God will always take us from faith to faith and from glory to glory if we allow Him to.

I discovered that because I chose to walk closely with Him, I have tapped into yet another dimension of prayer and intercession that I know is vital to the health of the body of Christ and the local church. After being trained and raised up in my local church house, I was appointed to be over the intercessors called **In-House Warriors**. Also, after being asked to be the conference speaker for our prophetic intercessors conference, I really felt the leading of the Holy Spirit to put into a book form the seminar that I did for the conference. The seminars theme was **"The In-House Warrior, God's Defense Mechanism."**

I immediately saw that the seminar was going to be a weapon that God uses to equip houses throughout the body of Christ in order to raise up and train intercessors. They will be intercessors equipped to thwart the plans of the enemy against the local church and the body of Christ as a whole. God used the conference to mightily equip us and to give us warfare strategies. Therefore, it is my prayer that this book will give an identity to the many who are already walking as intercessors and help to equip and train those that are being raised up as intercessors.

By no means does this book contain all that there is to know on the subject of 'weapons of mass destruction' to the kingdom of darkness, but I believe it is a good reference point; especially if you are just starting out. In the pages of this book, you will find out who you are and what God has set you up to defend in the body. **Intercession is a divine call that if called to it, you cannot escape it.** As an intercessor, prayer is in your belly; it is like a woman that is just waiting to give birth to whatever it is that heaven has assigned her to travail over. Just as our natural bodies have a defense mechanism to protect it from foreign bodies; we the intercessors all over Christendom are the defense mechanism that God uses to protect and defend that which is precious to Him — the Church! Intercessors are you ready?

Acknowledgement

First and foremost I would like to thank my Lord and Savior Jesus Christ for every gift that You have given me and for helping me to always know and understand that the gifts are not for me but for others. I love You Lord with every fiber of my being.

I want to thank my husband Sterling Smith for always supporting and encouraging me. I am truly a blessed woman and I thank God for you.

To every prayer warrior that took me under your wings over the years, I say thank you. There are just too many to name, but God knows who you are and this book is a fruit of your labor in my life. Truly without your mentorship I would not be where I am today.

And lastly to Dr. Mary O. and To His Glory Publishing: Words cannot begin to express the love that I have for you. Thank you for taking me under your wing and mentoring me and helping me to get these works published. You have been a blessing in my life in more ways than one and I look forward to many years of writing and publishing with you.

Chapter 1
Securing and Fortifying

A Word about Intercessors

In general, the intercessors are God's elite military force. Both individually and corporately, the "**Intercessor**" is a **Kingdom Weapon** that God is using to **reorganize** and **restructure** His Church in this current movement designed to secure and fortify the Church. The "**Intercessors**" secure and fortify the house (Church). In other words, through their intercession and warfare, the "set intercessors" of the house (men and women of God that are free from care) have the primary assignment to fortify, protect and strengthen the house against attack; they surround or provide the defensive spiritual military works needed in the house. Therefore, the "**Intercessors**" can be likened to members of U.S. Military Special Forces. In order for you to get a better picture of how the "**Intercessors**" secure and fortify their local churches, their homes, their cities and their nations, let us take a look at the elite military forces.

The U.S.'s Elite Military Force

The United States has special operation forces of the U. S. Military. These forces are designated by the United States Secretary of Defense and are specifically trained to conduct operations in an area that may be under enemy, unfriendly control, or politically sensitive environments. These forces are charged with the purpose of achieving military, diplomatic, informational and economic objectives of the United States.

These Special Forces soldiers are highly trained and are masters in areas of parachuting, swimming, and they are survival experts. They are also called the 'elite forces' and 'special action groups' that are usually sent to conduct search and rescue missions and on intelligence gathering inside enemy lines.

Intercessors as God's Special Forces

In parallel to that, the **Commander in Chief of the Universe, God Himself** has designated and anointed you and me as the "**Intercessors**" and we are specifically trained to conduct operations through our prayers and warfare in the spirit realm so that the agenda of the Kingdom will be realized on this earth as it is in heaven.

Just like the U.S. Special Forces, the "**Intercessors**" are highly trained in the Word of God which is their greatest weapon. They too are masters at parachuting, swimming, and they are also survival experts. Let me explain what I mean by this. The "**Intercessor**" has a built in parachute called **worship**. Like the Eagle, they are able to ascend into a high place and the heavenly realms. Unlike the jumper that has to be physically taken to a high place and then released, the Prayer Warrior has already been released by God. God's intercessors have many advantages over earthly Special Forces. For example, "**Intercessors**" do not have to be taken to a high place to get there.

"Intercessors" are able to ascend (pray) while driving a car, while walking in the park, while taking a shower, while reading a book, while sitting by the river; does anybody feel me? "Intercessors" can go to a high place without any external influence. What is in them will carry them to higher heights. From this high place, they are able to see what God is doing, and to hear what God is saying so that they can then secure and fortify through their prayers and warfare.

Special Forces utilize water to their advantage during their missions; and let me tell you that, **"Intercessors"** also like to hang around the water! The water allows Special Forces to infiltrate without being detected. In the Bible, fresh spring water or a river represents the Holy Spirit and the power of the Holy Spirit causes the **"Intercessor"** to infiltrate in order to secure and fortify. To the **"intercessor,"** the river serves as a natural visualization of a 'prophetic symbol' that speaks volumes. And yes, the **"Intercessor"** knows how to survive; we understand that in the secret place of the Most High God (in His presence), we get strategies and insight that we use to target our prayers and warfare. These prayers help us gain victory over the enemy so that the things and people that God has called us to preserve can survive!

Just like the Special Forces, we go in behind enemy lines to conduct rescue missions. Through our warfare, we literally pluck people up from the pits of hell. With the weapons of our warfare which are mighty (the whole armor of God) and the Hand of God Himself upon us, we are an elite group just like the Special Forces who have been called to shake wickedness and wreak havoc on the kingdom of darkness.

God's Team of Twelve (12)

Now, I have to take a side bar for a moment.

Something struck me when I was researching this topic and as simple as it may seem on the surface, I believe that it is prophetic in nature and it stirred me. I pray that it will stir you also to desire more of the prophetic flow. In my research I found that many elite teams are organized in teams of 12. Listen, there is a biblical principle and a prophetic insight to be gained here; the world is using it and does not even realize it.

Twelve (12) is a perfect number signifying <u>perfection of government or divine government and it has to do with the Apostolic rule</u>. The primary reason these elite forces go into other territories in most cases, is to deal with the lack of a proper governmental structure in the places. Therefore, to restore governmental rule or structure, these twelve are the first ones sent to do counterterrorism, direct action, foreign internal defense, special reconnaissance or unconventional warfare.

Listen, the Bible also uses 12 in a team. For example, there were twelve tribes of Israel, Jesus had twelve Apostles who were his closest followers, the Kingdom of God has twelve gates guarded by twelve angels and Jesus was twelve when he first appeard in public and spoke his first recorded words. These are just a few. Okay, the side bar is over and I pray you were able to pull some spiritual truths.

"Intercessors," we have been strategically placed to strike against an adversary whose primary goal is to steal, kill and destroy. Through our intercession and our warfare, we can prevent, deter, abort, raid, ambush, sabotage, subvert, strike, prepare, and train all God's children with the purpose of securing and fortifying. Therefore, intercessors, as soldiers in the Lord's army, I call you to "Attention!"

Chapter 2
Leaders Arm Yourselves

Strategy Defined

God is a God of the strategy. What do I mean by that? I think in order to understand the statement, we need to first define the word **strategy**. In the Hebrew language, it is the word **etsah**, which translated means **advice**, **consultation**, **counsel**, **designs**, **plans**, and **purpose**. So, God is a God of advice, consultation, counsel, designs, and plans. In other words, in everything that God has for us to do and accomplish in the Kingdom, he advises us on how to accomplish it, consults with us and gives us counsel on exactly what to do. He will give us the designs and plan or plans to get things done for His glory.

God has one goal or aim and that is, "that none should perish." To accomplish this, He is very direct in telling us what to do and how to defend His Kingdom in order to save those that are lost. He is a God of the "STRATEGY."

God's Strategy Used by Abraham

I truly believe that from natural pictures, we can pull spiritual truths or principles as we are told in 1 Corinthians 15:46. Therefore, in explaining how leaders are to arm themselves with an intercessory team, I want to look at a text of scripture in the book of Genesis. I believe that this particular text gives us a "God Strategy" for leaders on how to build strong intercessory teams within our local churches.

Genesis 14:1-16 (King James Version)

"¹ And it came to pass in the days of Amraphel king of Shinar, Arioch king of Ellasar, Chedorlaomer king of Elam, and Tidal king of nations;

² That these made war with Bera king of Sodom, and with Birsha king of Gomorrah, Shinab king of Admah, and Shemeber king of Zeboiim, and the king of Bela, which is Zoar.

³ All these were joined together in the vale of Siddim, which is the salt sea.

⁴Twelve years they served Chedorlaomer, and in the thirteenth year they rebelled.

⁵ And in the fourteenth year came Chedorlaomer, and the kings that were with him, and smote the Rephaims in Ashteroth Karnaim, and the Zuzims in Ham, and the Emins in Shaveh Kiriathaim,

⁶ And the Horites in their mount Seir, unto Elparan, which is by the wilderness.

⁷ And they returned, and came to Enmishpat, which is Kadesh, and smote all the country of the Amalekites, and also the Amorites, that dwelt in Hazezontamar.

⁸ And there went out the king of Sodom, and the king of Gomorrah, and the king

of Admah, and the king of Zeboiim, and the king of Bela (the same is Zoar;) and they joined battle with them in the vale of Siddim;

⁹ With Chedorlaomer the king of Elam, and with Tidal king of nations, and Amraphel king of Shinar, and Arioch king of Ellasar; four kings with five.

¹⁰ And the vale of Siddim was full of slimepits; and the kings of Sodom and Gomorrah fled, and fell there; and they that remained fled to the mountain.

¹¹ And they took all the goods of Sodom and Gomorrah, and all their victuals, and went their way.

¹² **And they took Lot, Abram's brother's son, who dwelt in Sodom, and his goods, and departed.**

¹³ And there came one that had escaped, and told Abram the Hebrew; for he dwelt in the plain of Mamre the Amorite, brother of Eshcol, and brother of Aner: and these were confederate with Abram.

¹⁴ **And when Abram heard that his brother was taken captive, he armed his trained servants, born in his own house, three hundred and eighteen, and pursued them unto Dan.**

¹⁵ **And he divided himself against them, he and his servants, by night, and smote them, and pursued them unto Hobah, which is on the left hand of Damascus.**

¹⁶ **And he brought back all the goods, and also brought again his brother Lot, and his goods, and the women also, and the people."**

In this passage of scripture, we find out that Lot; Abraham's brother's son was living in Sodom. Sodom came under attack and everything and everyone that lived in Sodom were taken captive. However, there was one person that escaped and that was able to get to Abraham and let him know what had happened to Lot and his family.

God's Strategy for Leaders

What happened next is a vital key to the strategy that God was putting in place for the leaders of today to follow. The text goes on to say that Abraham **"armed his trained servants, <u>born in his own house</u>, three hundred and eighteen (318)"** and they went and pursued them. This is where I want to park for a minute.

Genesis 13:5-9 tells us that Abraham was rich in cattle, in silver and in gold. His substance was so great that the land could not bear him and Lot together, so he must have had more than <u>318 men</u> in his house:

Genesis 13:5-9 (King James Version)

"⁵ And Lot also, which went with Abram, had flocks, and herds, and tents.

⁶ And the land was not able to bear them, that they might dwell together: for their substance was great, so that they could not dwell together.

⁷And there was a strife between the herd-men of Abram's cattle and the herdmen of Lot's cattle: and the Canaanite and the Perizzite dwelled then in the land.

⁸ And Abram said unto Lot, Let there be no strife, I pray thee, between me and thee, and between my herdmen and thy herdmen; for we be brethren.

⁹ Is not the whole land before thee? separate thyself, I pray thee, from me: if thou wilt take the left hand, then I will go to the right; or if thou depart to the right hand, then I will go to the left."

Chapter 3
Birthing the Intercessors

Intercessors that are Birthed in the House

Also, we know that there were men in Abraham's house that were <u>not born in his house</u> because in Genesis 17:27, it says, "….along with all the other men and boys of the household, <u>whether they were born there or bought as servants</u>. All were circumcised with him," yet the Bible is specific in pointing out that Abraham took these <u>specific 318</u> men. What was so special about these men verses the rest? The scripture text answers this question as well. They were servants born in Abraham's own house (hold that thought).

In Genesis 14, Abraham was about to go up against some heavy weights and he needed <u>the best of the best to have his back</u>. He needed to know that those standing with him were really standing with him. There was no time for anyone to go AWOL, DESERT, or even BETRAY him. But, because these 318 were birthed in his house, he knew the caliber of warriors that he had and that the previous description would not be their commentary. He had watched these young men be born into this world, run around as toddlers, grow in strength, develop into young warriors, and become men of valor; all under his watch. He knew their integrity and character, their strengths and weakness, but most of all, he knew of their loyalty to him and to the vision.

As we continue to read the text, we see that Abraham and his trained servants were successful in retrieving Lot, the people and their goods, plus some. Leaders, this is where your intercessory teams come into play. Within the Apostolic and Prophetic local houses, God is calling the leaders of these houses to raise up those 'born in the house' to take up arms of prayer, warfare and intercession to defend or **SHAMAR** the house. Genesis 2:15 is where we first see this word **SHAMAR** used. God put man in the Garden of Eden "to dress it and to **keep**" the Garden.

Genesis 2:15-17 (King James Version)

> "¹⁵ And the LORD God took the man, and put him into the Garden of Eden to dress it and to **keep** it."

That word **"keep"** is the Hebrew word **"Shamar."** It means <u>to hedge about as with thorns, to guard, to protect, to watch, to keep, to watch over, to stand guard over, to police, to secure, to shield, to shelter, to screen, to cover, to cloak, to preserve, to save, to conserve, to supervise, to keep under surveillance or control, to keep under guard, to govern, to restrain, to suppress, to be alert or to take care</u>. This is exactly what the trained servants of Abraham's house did. They helped to save Lot; to secure him, the people and all of their goods. They helped to suppress the enemy and preserve the life of Lot.

In the heat of the battle, Abraham could not afford to have anyone on the team defect just as the men and women of God cannot afford to have anyone on their team defect. Defectors are renegades; they rebel and lead revolts. They desert a cause in order to adopt another cause and they usually take folks with them. Does anyone remember an angel by the name of Lucifer?

Leaders need those that they have seen move from birth to maturity, to purpose, and to destiny as their intercessors. These are people that will remain loyal and have their leader's full circumference and not just their back; truly their full circumference! Leaders have a great responsibility and a mandate from God to fulfill the great commission. It is Satan's prime objective to keep them from fulfilling this commission.

Matthew 28:18-20 (King James Version)

> "[18] And Jesus came and spake unto them, saying, All power is given unto me in heaven and in earth.
>
> [19] Go ye therefore, and teach all nations, baptizing them in the name of the Father, and of the Son, and of the Holy Ghost:
>
> [20] Teaching them to observe all things whatsoever I have commanded you: and, lo, I am with you always, even unto the end of the world. Amen."

There will always be attacks, plots and schemes from the enemy until the return of Jesus Christ, but one of the strategies God uses to combat, defuse, thwart, demobilize and neutralize these devices is the **intercessor**.

Intercessors that are Birthed Outside the House

Before I end this chapter, I want to touch on another dimension of raising up teams of intercessors because I often found myself in this position as a result of being a military family and in constant transition. There are many people in Christendom that may be in a house that they were not birthed in (raised up in as men and women of God or intercessors), just as it was in Abraham's house concerning those who were not born there.

We noted in Genesis 17:27 that some of the males in Abraham's house were born in his house while others were bought as servants. Nevertheless, according to the text, they were all circumcised with Abraham. Although some were foreigners, they put aside what they believed or were previously taught and followed the example of their leader and were obedient to his instruction to become circumcised.

Today, we know that when the Word of God speaks of circumcision to us who are Christians, it is not literal but rather a cutting away of the things in our heart that are not pure and clean; a cutting away of sin. So, in retrospect to this picture in Genesis, an intercessor that was not raised in a certain ministry can become an intercessor in that ministry but only after there has been a cleansing or renewing of their mindset and their old way of doing things in their old houses of worship. We are admonished in Romans 12:1 not to be conformed, but to be transformed by the renewing of our minds.

Once these new intercessors have gone through the proper training and instruction, they can become a vital part of the team. Those that have a pure heart will usually easily make the transition. But those who are not emptied quickly can become just like a real OUT HOUSE and STINK!

When they stink, they have their own agenda and will usually not submit to the God ordained authority but set out to divide and conquer the team. They may operate under the influence of the Jezebel spirit; which hates the prophets of God or anything prophetic. In an instance like this, the leaders will have to determine the best course of action to take in order to neutralize the odor from the OUT HOUSE.

Another Example of One Birthed Outside the House

In the **book of Ruth** we can find a clear picture of someone birthed outside of the house and transformed. Ruth is a very familiar story but let us just recap it a bit. Ruth and Orpah were sisters married to the sons of Naomi. Ruth and Orpah were actually the daughters of the Moabite King which made them princesses. They both married Israelites and lived in the house of Naomi for about ten years. Naomi's husband had died some years before and then, both of her sons also died. As a result of losing her husband and sons, she decided to go back to Judah.

She urged both of her daughters-in-laws to go back to their own country but they were reluctant. Nevertheless, at her persistence, Orpah decided to return to her people and Naomi urged Ruth to follow after her and also return to her own country and to her own gods but Ruth had a different spirit. During those ten years of being a part of Naomi's family, she had been transformed and her mind had been renewed. Scripture records these words from Ruth:

Ruth 1: 16-18 (King James Version)

"[16] But Ruth replied, "Don't urge me to leave you or to turn back from you. Where you go I will go, and where you stay I will stay. Your people will be my people and your God my God.

[17] Where you die I will die, and there I will be buried. May the LORD deal with me, be it ever so severely, if anything but death separates you and me.

[18] When Naomi realized that Ruth was determined to go with her, she stopped urging her."

Ruth was saying look, I have been in your house for 10 years and what I knew before then is no longer my desire. My life is not that old life anymore; it was good but this is better. Do not make me go back; I want what I have seen you with in these last 10 years. Something greater has sustained you and caused you to be able to endure and rise above all of the adversity. That is what I want. The girl was BAD, (Boldly, Apprehending Destiny) and did not even know it; somebody say, 'BUT GOD!'

In essence, she told her; look, your God is now my God. This is a picture of someone birthed outside the house but has become transformed and sold out to the house! Orpah on the other hand, was just glad to be free to go back and do her thing. After 10 years of sitting at the feet of this woman of God, I was perplexed that she gave in to Naomi's urges to return to her people while Ruth did not. I submit here that she never made the full transition to the ways of the house that she was in; the 'Out' was still in her.

My theory is supported by the research that I conducted in the Jewish Women Encyclopedia *(http:// jwa.org/encyclopedia/article/orpah-midrash-and-aggadah)* that states the following:

"Orpah's departure from Naomi is seen as proper and she and her offspring were rewarded for the considerable way that she accompanied Naomi (BT Sotah 42b). However, once she had taken her leave of her mother-in-law, her subsequent actions are deemed extremely negative. She is said to have lain, that very night, with one hundred men, and even with a dog.

The Philistine Goliath, who fought the young David during the battle in the valley of Elah, was born of this promiscuous activity. (Ruth Rabbah 2:20). Orpah's wanton behavior is said to be characteristic of her and one of the exegeses of her name describes such conduct: "Orpah—because everyone ground her like bruised corn [harifot]" (BT Sotah loc. cit.).

Be rest assured that eventually, an OUT HOUSE will stink. It may be 2 weeks or 2 years, but what is in the heart when given the opportunity to show itself forth, will come out. Below is the full narration of the story of Orpah, Naomi and Ruth:

Ruth 1:1-22 (King James Version)

"1 Now it came to pass in the days when the judges ruled, that there was a famine in the land. And a certain man of Bethlehemjudah went to sojourn in the country of Moab, he, and his wife, and his two sons.

2 And the name of the man was Elimelech, and the name of his wife Naomi, and the name of his two sons Mahlon and Chilion, Ephrathites of Bethlehemjudah. And they came into the country of Moab, and continued there.

3 And Elimelech Naomi's husband died; and she was left, and her two sons.

4 And they took them wives of the women of Moab; the name of the one was Orpah, and the name of the other Ruth: and they dwelled there about ten years.

5 And Mahlon and Chilion died also both of them; and the woman was left of her two sons and her husband.

6 Then she arose with her daughters in law, that she might return from the country of Moab: for she had heard in the country of Moab how that the LORD had visited his people in giving them bread.

7 Wherefore she went forth out of the place where she was, and her two daughters in law with her; and they went on the way to return unto the land of Judah.

8 And Naomi said unto her two daughters in law, Go, return each to her mother's house: the LORD deal kindly with you, as ye have dealt with the dead, and with me.

9 The LORD grant you that ye may find rest, each of you in the house of her husband. Then she kissed them; and they lifted up their voice, and wept.

10 And they said unto her, Surely we will return with thee unto thy people.

11 And Naomi said, Turn again, my daughters: why will ye go with me? are there yet any more sons in my womb, that they may be your husbands?

12 Turn again, my daughters, go your way; for I am too old to have an husband. If I should say, I have hope, if I should have an husband also to night, and should also bear sons;

13 Would ye tarry for them till they were grown? would ye stay for them from

having husbands? nay, my daughters; for it grieveth me much for your sakes that the hand of the LORD is gone out against me.

[14] And they lifted up their voice, and wept again: and Orpah kissed her mother in law; but Ruth clave unto her.

[15] And she said, Behold, thy sister in law is gone back unto her people, and unto her gods: return thou after thy sister in law.

[16] And Ruth said, Intreat me not to leave thee, or to return from following after thee: for whither thou goest, I will go; and where thou lodgest, I will lodge: thy people shall be my people, and thy God my God:

[17] Where thou diest, will I die, and there will I be buried: the LORD do so to me, and more also, if ought but death part thee and me.

[18] When she saw that she was stedfastly minded to go with her, then she left speaking unto her.

[19] So they two went until they came to Bethlehem. And it came to pass, when they were come to Bethlehem, that all the city was moved about them, and they said, Is this Naomi?

20 And she said unto them, Call me not Naomi, call me Mara: for the Almighty hath dealt very bitterly with me.

21 I went out full and the LORD hath brought me home again empty: why then call ye me Naomi, seeing the LORD hath testified against me, and the Almighty hath afflicted me?

22 So Naomi returned, and Ruth the Moabitess, her daughter in law, with her, which returned out of the country of Moab: and they came to Bethlehem in the beginning of barley harvest."

Leaders, you need personal intercessors! The higher you move up in the ranks as a Christian Leader, the higher you move up on the devil's hit list. To be specific, when you reach levels of five-fold ministry, spiritual warfare will become more intense. This is why the Apostle Paul's heart was very compassionate to the other leaders in his days that he called "true yokefellow" as we see below:

Philippians 4:3 (King James Version)

"3 And I intreat thee also, true yokefellow, help those women which laboured with me in the gospel, with Clement also, and with other my fellowlabourers, whose names are in the book of life."

I heard a well know Apostle of our day say something to the effect of, every leader is personally responsible for putting on the full armor of God but such individual protection may not suffice in every case. It is a necessary starting point, but there is <u>more</u>. Leaders, the "more" this Apostle was speaking of are those in the body that God has given the spiritual gift of intercession to. Some of these intercessors have been given an assignment and are called to stand in the gap for their Christian leaders.

I can tell you from personal experience that this is true. There have been times when God has had me on such an assignment. During these times and on many occasions, God alerted me to the attacks that the enemy was plotting against my leaders. Once, the Lord showed me my leader collapsing and then announcing that they were going to have surgery. I immediately began to intercede and pray against this attack. I never said a word to my leader; I only shared it with my husband for him to be in agreement with me and it was because the Lord allowed me to share it with him.

Sometime later, my leader shared with me before it was shared with the congregation that they were going to have surgery but I believe that because of the intercession, the blow that the enemy was planning to deliver was not as severe as the enemy had hoped. This leader had surgery without any complications and was back up and ministering within a few weeks.

Leaders, if you have **Seers** in your houses or those prophetic watchman type intercessors, God has placed them there for a reason. God will show you who your Peter, James and John are.

Chapter 4
Defending the House

Definition of the House

Even today, the gates of hell are attempting to prevail against the Church still, but Jesus let all of heaven and earth know in Matthew 16:18 that the gates of hell shall not prevail against the Church.

Matthew 16:18 (King James Version)

> "¹⁸ And I say also unto thee, That thou art Peter, and upon this rock I will build my church; and the gates of hell shall not prevail against it."

The **Church** in this verse is the Greek word **Ekklesia** which means:

1. A gathering of citizens called out from their homes into some public place.

2. An assembly of the people convened at the public place of the council for the purpose of deliberating.

3. An assembly of Christians gathered for worship in a religious meeting.

4. A company of Christians or of those who are hoping for eternal salvation through Jesus Christ; observe their own religious rites, hold their own religious meetings,

and manage their own affairs according to regulations prescribed for the body for order's sake.

5. Those who anywhere in a city or village constitute such a company and are united into one body:

   a) The whole body of Christians scattered throughout the earth.
   b) The assembly of faithful Christians already dead and received into heaven.

We, the believers of today are the **Ekklesia**, the called out ones and when we come together in a public place, this is what makes up the House of God. **House** is the Greek word **Oikos** which means:

1. An inhabited house, home

2. Any building whatsoever

   a) Of a palace

   b) The house of God, the tabernacle

   c) The family of God, of the Christian Church, of the church of the Old and New Testaments

So, not only is the enemy trying to prevail against you and me individually, but he is trying to prevail against the House of God collectively. Therefore, as intercessors, it is our job to "Defend the House."

Defending Our Family — Physically

One of the definitions of the house was an inhabited house or home. In layman's terms, a house is the physical place where you and I live. Many of us have spouses and children or maybe you live alone, but at any rate, your number one priority for your house and those in your house is keeping everyone safe physically from intruders. We as consumers spend millions of dollars each year defending our houses from burglary.

We want to make sure that our loved ones are safe while relaxing in the comfort of our homes and while we are asleep in our homes. We invest in systems like ADT, some have fire arms (I am not advocating you do this), while others have high-tech video surveillance installed. Whatever method of security you choose, the common goal is to stop intruders from being able to come in and do harm to you and to your loved ones.

Another way we defend our houses physically, is protecting the actual structure; the house itself. Each year across the nation, homes are not only damaged by an occasional storm but by some very small but dangerous pest; yes, termites. Termites are not the only pest that we have to defend our homes against because there are roaches and other rodents that seek to invade and take over.

In my case, I know that we have a plan with a company and they come out monthly and inspect and spray to prevent these types of pests and rodents from ever setting up camp. It is important to be proactive and not reactive when it comes to protecting and defending our homes. Being reactive can end up costing us thousands of dollars, while being proactive can save us even more thousands of dollars.

And lastly, we defend our homes by protecting our possessions within our homes; like our furniture, or appliances and so forth. If you had a leak in your roof, you would not allow that leak to go unrepaired. The cost to replace carpet and furniture would far outweigh the cost of simply fixing the leak on the roof. Sometimes, homeowners see small things that need repairing but figure they have time and put off simple inexpensive repairs. Over a period of time and most often when it is too late, that simple penny to fix repairs turns into thousands of dollars in makeovers that frustrate and disrupt our lives and our budgets.

Defending the Saints in the House — Spiritually

Not only do we as believers have our natural family, we also have our spiritual family; those of the same faith, our common denominator being our Lord and Savior Jesus Christ. Just as we have different defense mechanisms in place to protect our houses, guess what, God has His defense mechanism in place as well.

We first defend the house by "**Shamaring**" the people in the house of God. Yes, our brothers and sisters in Christ. As **intercessors,** we have to defend the laity. To help you understand this concept, let us look at Genesis chapter 4. In this text, Adam and Eve have two sons, <u>Cain</u> and <u>Abel</u>. Abel was a keeper of the sheep, but Cain was a tiller of the ground. They both made offerings to the Lord but <u>God did not receive the offering Cain gave but he received Abel's offering</u>.

Now, Cain in his anger and rage killed his brother, Abel. In verse nine, God asked Cain where his brother Abel was and <u>Cain replied with</u>, "Am I my brother's keeper?"

Genesis 4:1-12 (King James Version)

"¹ And Adam knew Eve his wife; and she conceived, and bare Cain, and said, I have gotten a man from the LORD.

² And she again bare his brother Abel. And Abel was a keeper of sheep, but Cain was a tiller of the ground.

³ And in process of time it came to pass, that Cain brought of the fruit of the ground an offering unto the LORD.

⁴ And Abel, he also brought of the firstlings of his flock and of the fat thereof. And the LORD had respect unto Abel and to his offering:

⁵ But unto Cain and to his offering he had not respect. And Cain was very wroth, and his countenance fell.

⁶ And the LORD said unto Cain, Why art thou wroth? and why is thy countenance fallen?

⁷ If thou doest well, shalt thou not be accepted? and if thou doest not well, sin lieth at the door. And unto thee shall be his desire, and thou shalt rule over him.

⁸ And Cain talked with Abel his brother: and it came to pass, when they were in the field, that Cain rose up against Abel his brother, and slew him.

⁹ And the LORD said unto Cain, Where is Abel thy brother? And he said, I know not: Am I my brother's keeper

¹⁰ The LORD said, "What have you done? Listen! Your brother's blood cries out to me from the ground.

¹¹ Now you are under a curse and driven from the ground, which opened its mouth to receive your brother's blood from your hand.

¹² When you work the ground, it will no longer yield its crops for you. You will be a restless wanderer on the earth."

Again, that word **keeper** in Hebrew is the word **shamar**. So, <u>Cain was saying am I supposed to stand guard over him, protect him, defend him, shield him, preserve, save and take care of him</u>? The Lord responded with, "What have you done?" In other words, yes Cain, you were supposed to **shamar** your brother. And if you read on, you will see the fate of Cain for not **shamaring** his very own brother. I submit to you **intercessors** that in defending the house, we are to **shamar** our brothers and sisters in our house.

What ADT and security cameras are to the world, we the **intercessors** are to the house. We are in covenant with God and our leaders to **shamar** the people of God. Intercessors, God has a great interest in the health and well being of His people. He said that above all, He wants His children to prosper and be in good health. In like manner, Leaders are to be greatly concerned about the health and well being of the people God has called them to shepherd and we are to follow the example that is set before us. We have to love the church and by that I mean the people; we are our brothers' keepers.

We love the people we live with right...? Then, we've got to love the people we assemble with. Intercessors, when we do not "**Shamar**" the people, here are a list of some things that can happen:

1. Accidents
2. Apathy
3. Backsliding
4. Broken relationships
5. Confusion
6. Conspiracies
7. Divorces and separations
8. Family problems
9. Financial attacks
10. Immorality
11. Stagnation
12. Unexplainable sickness and diseases

13. Wolves entering the flock and warlocks
14. Witches entering the flock and divination

Intercessors, take up arms and "**Shamar**" the people!

Defending Against Pests in the House

Just as we have pests in our natural houses, we have pests in the house of God too. There is nothing more frustrating than a <u>gossiping pest</u>. There are many more but this pest within the Church can do a lot of harm if not dealt with swiftly.

Definition of Gossip

> **Gossip** is derived from the idea of <u>whispering</u>. According to Dictionary. com, "**gossip**" means to indulge in talk or rumors about others; spreading of sensational stories or malicious talk about others."

The Apostle Paul spoke strongly against idle talks and gossip as we see in the scripture below. It opens the doors to the enemy in God's house:

1 Timothy 5:12-14 (New King James Version)

> "12 having condemnation because they have cast off their first faith.

> 13 And besides they learn to be idle, wandering about from house to house, and not only idle but also gossips and busybodies, saying things which they ought not.

14 Therefore I desire that the younger widows marry, bear children, manage the house, give no opportunity to the adversary to speak reproachfully."

Also, the following scriptures speak against gossip:

Proverbs 11:12-13 (New Living Translation)

"12 It is foolish to belittle one's neighbor; a sensible person keeps quiet."

13 A gossip goes around telling secrets, but those who are trustworthy can keep a confidence."

Proverbs 20:19 (New Living Translation)

"19 A gossip goes around telling secrets, so don't hang around with chatterers."

Romans 1:28-30 (New Living Translation)

"28 Since they thought it foolish to acknowledge God, he abandoned them to their foolish thinking and let them do things that should never be done.

29 Their lives became full of every kind of wickedness, sin, greed, hate, envy, murder, quarreling, deception, malicious behavior, and gossip.

³⁰ They are backstabbers, haters of God, insolent, proud, and boastful. They invent new ways of sinning, and they disobey their parents."

1 Timothy 5:13 (New Living Translation)

"¹³ And if they are on the list, they will learn to be lazy and will spend their time gossiping from house to house, meddling in other people's business and talking about things they shouldn't."

Proverbs 16:28 (New Living Translation)

"²⁸ A troublemaker plants seeds of strife; gossip separates the best of friends."

Gossip is very dangerous because it is so subtle. Some areas of gossip that scriptures deal with and that we (Intercessors) need to war against are **busybodies** (2 Thessalonians 3:11; 1 Timothy 5:13), **talebearers** (Proverbs 26:20; Proverbs 11:13), **slanderers** (Proverbs 10:18; Jeremiah 6:28), **evil whispering** (Proverbs 16:28; Romans 1:29), **evil speaking** (Ephesians 4:31; 1 Peter 2:1), and **backbiting** (Romans 1: 30).

Now, it is not our job to police people. We should never approach people and say to them you are a busybody or talebearer and so forth. We watch and pray because it is not the person, but a spirit operating through the person. Remember, we're not dealing with flesh and blood. Unless you have been delegated authority by your leader to confront and deal, then you watch and pray.

Defending our Possessions in the House

When I talk about defending our possessions in the house of God, the connotation is not so much material things. Although we do defend the possessions in our homes against being burglarized by adopting the same method of protection that we do in protecting our personal homes, more than anything, my focus is the spiritual possessions in the house of God. Possessions deals with ownership and we must take ownership of the ministries within the house of God.

As **intercessors**, we need to "**Shamar**" the ministries within the house. There are many ministries within the local Church and they all need to be covered in prayer but there is one that Satan seems to target to a greater degree and that is, <u>Praise and Worship</u>. We are going to get into Praise and Worship in another chapter but we must pray and intercede for the various auxiliaries and ministries in our houses.

Chapter 5
Defending Our Leaders

Attacks Against Leaders

When we talk about defending our leaders, we are still in a **SHAMAR** mode but the level of warfare that we engage in may be more intense since if you cut the head off, the rest of the body will die. So, it does not surprise me at all that in 1 Timothy 2:1-3 we are instructed to make supplications, prayers, intercessions and giving of thanks for our leaders. They need this from all the saints; but especially, from the **intercessors.**

1 Timothy 2:1-3 (King James Version)

> "¹ I exhort therefore, that, first of all, supplications, prayers, intercessions, and giving of thanks, be made for all men;
>
> ²For kings, and for all that are in authority; that we may lead a quiet and peaceable life in all godliness and honesty.
>
> ³ For this is good and acceptable in the sight of God our Saviour."

I want to focus on two areas that the enemy will use to attack leaders. I call them **internal attacks** and **external attacks**. I want to start this discussion by using the Customer Service Training Class in my workplace as an illustration of internal and external influences.

In my workplace, we are required to take Customer Service training annually. In our customer service classes, we always talk about "Internal" and "External" customers. Your internal customers are the people you work with on a day to day basis. You actually spend more time with them than you do your family.

Your external customers are the people that come into your place of work that you provide services to. **We spend more time in our customer service training classes dealing with issues from internal customers than we do dealing with issues from our external customers! It would seem that it would be the exact opposite**.

<u>It has been my personal experience that my internal customers have often times caused me more grief than my external customers</u>. This grief usually comes in the form of betrayal. External customers usually come in already disgruntled over something that does not have anything to do with me. Therefore, when they come off brash, I do not take it so personal. They are just having a bad day; it has nothing to do with me.

Over the years, I have witnessed betrayal not only in the workplace, but in the house of God as well. Specifically, with the leaders being the ones betrayed. King David said it like this…

Psalm 55:12-14 (New International Version)

> "[12] If an enemy were insulting me, I could endure it; if a foe were raising himself against me, I could hide from him.
>
> [13] But it is you, a man like myself, my companion, my close friend,

¹⁴ with whom I once enjoyed sweet fellow-ship as we walked with the throng at the house of God."

Wow, David said if an enemy were insulting me (an external customer), I could handle it but it is not somebody off the street that I really do not know that is betraying me but a close friend (an internal customer); someone with whom I spend time and that I think I really know. There are many 'Davids' in the body of Christ that are being betrayed and we as **intercessors** have to **SHAMAR** them as men and women of God.

Defending Against Internal Attacks

Some of the spirits to be on the lookout for and to war against internally are Absolom, Korah, Joab, Levithian, Sabatoge, and Judas. Let us take a brief look at a few of these and see why they are internal.

1. **Absolom (2 Samuel 13:1-19:8)**

   Absolom was King David's son and he rebelled against his father. Remember, we are talking about underlined internal attacks against our leaders. It is sad to say but many sons and daughters are rebelling against God's ordained leaders.

   Those who walk in a spirit of Absolom will display some specific traits. These are some of the signs, symptoms and manifestations of this spirit: betrayal, conspiracy, cunning craftiness, deception, defiance, diabolical alliance, disrespect, divided allegiance, haughtiness, jealousy, lust, lying, rebellion, sedition, seduction, treason, undermining ministry and its influence, usurping authority, hostility, hypocrisy and irreverence.

In order to combat this spirit, intercessors need to release into the atmosphere; a spirit of submission, a spirit of humility, a spirit of integrity and for this person to have the heart of a servant, the peace and truth of God.

2. **Korah (Numbers 16:1-19)**
   Korah was a leader in Israel (Internal customer). He was a Levite who helped with the daily duties in the Tabernacle. Korah incited his own rebellion and recruited others in leadership. Korah along with the other leaders confronted Moses and Aaron with their list of complaints. The summary of the first thing Korah said was:

   • You are no better than anyone else

   • Everyone in Israel has been chosen of the Lord and

   • We do not need to obey you Moses. True, Moses was not better than anyone else and yes, all of Israel had been chosen to be God's people but his application of these truths was wrong. Moses was the person God chose and ordained as the Leader over Israel. The truth be told, Korah's desire to lead caused him to rebel and he not only lost his job, but his life as well.

When this spirit is in operation in the local Church, it will form unholy partnerships and it will convince subordinate leaders (internal customers) to rebel against God's divine authority (senior leaders) and against delegated authority. It does not want to give honor and respect to those that honor and respect are due because this spirit feels it is equal in rank and calling. Intercessors need to decree and declare that there will be order, proper protocol, and unity among the leaders in the house.

They need to further decree that leaders will have the mind of Christ and that they will walk in humility and stay in their lanes. As Intercessors, we have to cover the leaders of the house in prayer in order to defend them against these internal attacks!

Defending Against External Attacks

We correlated external attacks to that of a workplace where customers come in from the outside to receive services. Often times, customers come into places of business already on the defense and hostile; not because of something we have done, but because of something that happened before they arrived to our place of business. It is no different in the Church. Therefore, we as "Intercessors" have to "**Shamar**" our leaders from these types of attacks as well. Three key players in these types of external attacks are the Jezebel spirit, the Ahab spirit and the Python spirit. I want us to look for just a few moments at the Jezebel spirit.

Jezebel
Jezebel is a biblical character that you can read more about in 1 Kings 16. You are going to have to study this

one out because there is so much information about it and I just want to whet your appetite and provoke you to study this out. Jezebel was the daughter of Ethbaal who was the king and high priest over Baal worship. Jezebel married Ahab the king of Israel and she gained access to Israel's religious platform. She introduced the worship of Ashtoreth to Israel. She was not internal but external; yet, she gained access by attaching herself to someone who was internal and not to just any old body, but to someone who was in a high position of authority.

As a result of this, 10 million Israelites abandoned worshipping God and began to worship Baal and Ashtoreth. Only 7,000 people in the nation at that time were not persuaded by her to worship another god. Jezebel herself was not the spirit but the evil spirit now known by her name was influencing and controlling her. As a result, the spirit became identifiable by her name.

This spirit hates true spiritual authority and usually controls through manipulation. This spirit uses emotional pressure, witchcraft and sensuality to gain power. It comes in the house (external customer) of God and scans the room to find those people in the house that are in positions of authority and close to God's set man and woman of God. She/He will then try to get close to these individuals by means of flattery. I say to intercessors, look out for the flatterers as this should be an alarm to our spirit. This spirit is gender neutral but will often times present herself as a "prophetess." This spirit hates God's true prophets. Intercessors, loose the spirit of Jehu against the Jezebel Spirit.

Chapter 6
Pitfalls to Guard Against

There are three pitfalls that I want to target that **intercessors** should guard against.

1. Familiarity
The first pitfall is the pitfall of <u>familiarity</u>. What is familiarity? Dictionary.com defines it as:

- Considerable acquaintance with.
- Established friendship; intimacy.

Relationship is inevitable. In every area of our lives, we are going to enter into and engage in relationships. Over a period of time, some of these relationships will become more intimate than others and I do not mean intimate in a sexual way. The danger of this can be the familiarity piece of it. As **intercessor**, we will walk closely with God's set men and women of God. Many of you will be a part of the inner circle and you have to guard against the pitfall of familiarity. Let us look at some scriptures.

Jesus encountered familiarity during His earthly ministry. In Mark 1:1-6, we find Jesus in His home town. And as he was teaching, the people said, "Is not this the carpenter...?" They were not able to receive the fullness of all that He could have done that day. Only a few were healed because, for many of them, all they could see was Mary's son and not Joseph's son; whose lineage and genealogy was from King David and Abraham. Because of their familiarity, the many healings and miracles that I am sure Jesus wanted to do were hindered.

Mark 6:1-6 (King James Version)

"¹ And he went out from thence, and came into his own country; and his disciples follow him.

² And when the sabbath day was come, he began to teach in the synagogue: and many hearing him were astonished, saying, From whence hath this man these things? and what wisdom is this which is given unto him, that even such mighty works are wrought by his hands?

³ Is not this the carpenter, the son of Mary, the brother of James, and Joses, and of Juda, and Simon? and are not his sisters here with us? And they were offended at him.

⁴ But Jesus, said unto them, A prophet is not without honour, but in his own country, and among his own kin, and in his own house.

⁵ And he could there do no mighty work, save that he laid his hands upon a few sick folk, and healed them.

⁶ And he marvelled because of their unbelief. And he went round about the villages, teaching."

Familiarity can cause us not to be able to receive from our men and women of God in crucial times of our lives. It will also hinder the move of God not only in our lives, but in the lives of others that God may want to use us in. Familiarity can also cause you to move into an area of disrespect. This is a dangerous place to be in. As an **intercessor** you have to maintain that balance.

A famous philosopher cited four areas of familiarity that we should watch for.

- Committed
- Casual
- Cynical and finally
- Contempt

Let us take a look at these four areas. We start out committed to the cause and then as we interact with those to whom we have committed ourselves, formed considerable acquaintances, establish friendship and become intimate with them, we become casual; meaning that we can become nonchalant or become temporarily attached. This is the place where the relationship can take a twist for the worst. This is the area we need to make sure we keep balanced.

If we fail to keep this area balanced, then we will move into being cynical. When we become cynical we become sarcastic and question the motives of our leaders. If we ever reach this place, the next and final place is a place of contempt. When people reach this place, they scorn their leaders, they despise them, they disrespect them and they view them as unimportant voices in their lives. We need to quickly repent and realign ourselves if we ever fall into this pitfall.

2. **Displaced Loyalty**
   The second pitfall that we as intercessors need to guard against is displaced loyalty. Our loyalty should be to the Shepherd (Jesus) and not the sheep. The shepherd's job is to watch over the flock. If the leader is a true ordained and delegated shepherd of Jesus who is the great Shepherd Himself, the leader will not harm the sheep. He will know just what the sheep need. The Lord will download into his or her spirit everything that he or she needs to take care of God's people.

   Remember, one third of the angels fell and lost their first estate because they shifted their loyalty. There must be a mutual trust between you and your leaders. The Word of God declares that two cannot walk together unless they agree. You just need to make sure you are in agreement with the Shepherd and not the sheep. In the case of Lucifer, one third of the angels were so busy trying to impress their leader instead of remaining loyal to their Creator. We do not need to try and impress the people but we need to remain loyal to our leaders.

3. **Unhealthy Relationships**
   We as **intercessors** have to guard our

hearts and make sure that we enter into and maintain healthy relationships; especially within the house of God. The Bible says that "out of the abundance of the heart the mouth speaks" and that from the heart flows the "issues of life":

Luke 6:45 (King James Version)

"⁴⁵ A good man out of the good treasure of his heart bringeth forth that which is good; and an evil man out of the evil treasure of his heart bringeth forth that which is evil: for of the abundance of the heart his mouth speaketh."

Proverbs 4:23 (King James Version)

"²³ Keep thy heart with all diligence; for out of it are the issues of life."

First of all, people will have issues with you being an **intercessor** and they will always try to lure you away from your God ordained position. The enemy hates the prophetic and will attempt to stop the flow of the prophetic no matter what the cost to you and I are. You want to make sure that your relationships are divinely ordained by God.

Secondly, people will always have issues with God's ordained leaders and the enemy is bold and will use people to be very vocal about the issues that they may have with the men and women of God that you are defending as an **intercessor**. These may very well be people that we have relationships with and when this happens, we have to quickly terminate the relationships. Not terminating these relationships can be a major pitfall that the enemy is setting up against you as an **intercessor**.

As a wife, I am not going to remain in a relationship with someone who is slandering my husband and also as a mother, I am not going to remain in a relationship with someone who is slandering my children. Well, as sons and daughters in the Kingdom, we should not remain in relationships with people who are slandering our "Fathers and Mothers in the faith." We should be quick to defend them and in love, bring correction to those who are making railing accusations. Listen, the Bible is right, bad communication will eventually corrupt good character.

1 Corinthians 15:33 (King James Version)

"[33] Be not deceived: evil communications corrupt good manners."

You cannot even entertain the negative words or allow them to get into your spirit because all Satan needs is a foothold or just a little peep or crack to get in. We have to cast down arguments and every high thing that exalts itself against the knowledge of God. Do you know that when people slander God's ordained leaders, they exalt themselves against the knowledge of God? They are in essence saying that they know better than God who leads us all. It is a dangerous place to be and we must be the TERMINATORS and say, "Hasta la vista baby!" Hallelujah!:

2 Corinthians 10:4-6 (New King James Version)

"[4] For the weapons of our warfare are not carnal but mighty in God for pulling down strongholds,

[5] casting down arguments and every high thing that exalts itself against the knowledge of God, bringing every thought into captivity to the obedience of Christ,

[6] and being ready to punish all disobedience when your obedience is fulfilled."

Chapter 7
Defending the Vision

Before we can talk about <u>defending the vision</u>, let us talk about what the "**Vision**" is. The **vision** is a strategic plan God gives to each local church through His ordained leaders of that local body to fulfill the mandate that Jesus gave the Church in Matthew 28:18-20:

Matthew 28:18-20 (King James Version)

> "¹⁸ And Jesus came and spake unto them, saying, All power is given unto me in heaven and in earth.
>
> ¹⁹ Go ye therefore, and teach all nations, baptizing them in the name of the Father, and of the Son, and of the Holy Ghost:
>
> ²⁰ Teaching them to observe all things whatsoever I have commanded you: and, lo, I am with you always, even unto the end of the world. Amen."

This plan is divinely communicated through several vehicles like prophecy or visions. So, **intercessors,** why are we to defend the vision if God has given it to the leaders of the house? Let us dig in for answers.

In Habakkuk 2:1-4, we find the Prophet Habakkuk positioning himself to see what God was going to say to him and what he would answer. This Prophet is a picture of our leaders today. Just like the Prophet, our leaders set their watch to both see and hear what God is saying concerning their local houses. As the Prophet listened and as our leaders listen, the Lord answers.

The Lord instructed the Prophet Habakkuk to first write the vision or the strategic plan down and to make sure that what he writes is plain or understandable and not complicated. Why is this? The answer is so that he (that is you and I; the **intercessors**) may run when we read it. The Lord is still doing the same today; instructing our leaders as He downloads to them the strategies and plans for them to fulfill the Great Commission—to write it down and make it plain.

It is interesting that he did not tell them to write it down and make it plain so that they could read it and run with it, but the Lord is clear that someone else will be reading it and running with it. **Intercessors,** this is where you and I come in and we are to defend the vision. We are the "he" that will run. This does not mean that we will literally run, but it speaks of a messenger of the vision.

We are to be messengers of the vision of our various houses. Back then, they had runners that carried messages from one place to another and the runners not only carried the message, but they guarded it as they were carrying it. In other words, they protected it as if their lives depended upon it. That word **readeth**, means to call out, recite, cry out or proclaim.

Intercessors, our leaders are depending upon us and God has charged them to write the vision down. They in turn, then charge us to give not just voice to the vision but to carry and deliver the vision. What this means is that we are to recite it, cry it out, proclaim it and call it out while we guard and defend it.

Habakkuk 2:1-3 (King James Version)

"¹ I will stand upon my watch, and set me upon the tower, and will watch to see what he will say unto me, and what I shall answer when I am reproved.

² And the LORD answered me, and said, Write the vision, and make it plain upon tables, that he may run that readeth it.

³ For the vision is yet for an appointed time, but at the end it shall speak, and not lie: though it tarry, wait for it; because it will surely come, it will not tarry"

The vision of the local house is very important. First, it gets you on God's program and off your own. Everyone has an agenda, but the vision will help reel you in and make sure your focus is the agenda of the house. Listen, we do not need to even have an agenda because God assures us in His Word that our gifts will make room for us. We just need to wait on Him and while we wait, serve the vision of the house that we are in.

Proverbs 18:16 (King James Version)

"¹⁶ A man's gift maketh room for him, and bringeth him before great men."

Next, the vision gives the church a target. The reason for this is because, the vision pinpoints exactly what the goal is that we are trying to reach and how to go about accomplishing that goal. The enemy would like nothing more than to have us all shooting our arrows in different directions but if we all focus and shoot our arrows at the same thing, we can take it down!

Psalm 133:1-3 (King James Version)

"¹ Behold, how good and how pleasant it is for brethren to dwell together in unity!

² It is like the precious ointment upon the head, that ran down upon the beard, even Aaron's beard: that went down to the skirts of his garments;

³ As the dew of Hermon, and as the dew that descended upon the mountains of Zion: for there the LORD commanded the blessing, even life for evermore."

Lastly, the vision will get people into the game. For the most part leaders are in the game, but sometimes the saints are not active and involved. When they have a clear vision they will become excited about Kingdom work. **Intercessors,** we have to defend the vision of our local houses because as you have read, it affects everyone from the pulpit to the pews.

How to Defend the Vision

We have talked a lot about the vision and why it warrants defending but let us now talk about how we as **intercessors** go about doing that. The first line of defense is simply, knowing what the vision of your house is. You cannot defend something that you do not know yourself. And when I say know, I do not just mean something that you memorized. In school, we memorize a lot of things for test purposes, but we did not gain any understanding or comprehension of what we memorized. Therefore, what I am saying is that you have to understand or fully comprehend the vision of your house and you have to be able to articulate it to others.

Proverbs 4:7 (King James Version)

> "7 Wisdom is the principal thing; therefore get wisdom: and with all thy getting get understanding."

Defending the vision also means that you will have to sacrifice for the vision sometimes. In other words, there will be times that as an **intercessor**, you will have to lay some things down and sacrifice yourself and your stuff for the vision. Jesus understood this; the Father gave Jesus the vision for humanity and for His kingdom. To fulfill the vision, Jesus laid down His very life so that you and I might have eternal life. The beautiful thing about it all is that in His death, God won a great victory when He raised Him up again from the dead!

John 15:13 (King James Version)

> "13 Greater love hath no man than this, that a man lay down his life for his friends."

Intercessors, as we lay down and sacrifice our feelings, emotions, desires, affections, time, gifts, and talents to defend the vision, we know that dying to oneself will bring forth great victory for the vision.

Chapter 8
Defending the Gates

Gates in the Bible were the center of city life. Gates symbolize the entry way into a palace, a camp, a temple or a city. Gates were the only way to enter and exit the city. They provided the city with access to food, goods and sometimes even water. These gates consisted of two halves that were secured by strong locks. These gates had to be opened with a large key that was sometimes more than two feet in length.

Amos 5:10 (King James Version)

"¹⁰ They hate him that rebuketh in the gate, and they abhor him that speaketh uprightly."

Amos 5:15 (King James Version)

"¹⁵ Hate the evil, and love the good, and establish judgment in the gate: it may be that the LORD God of hosts will be gracious unto the remnant of Joseph."

Isaiah 22:22 (King James Version)

"²² And the key of the house of David will I lay upon his shoulder; so he shall open, and none shall shut; and he shall shut, and none shall open."

Also, gates represent authority, jurisdiction, dwelling, strength, power and dominion. The enemy has always been out to unseat that authority so that he can plunder the people and usurp our God-given authority for himself. Gates were the marketplace and gates were where the elders met. Kings also sat at the gates to meet people and to make legal decisions. The priests and prophets sometimes delivered their messages at the gates. This explains why Amos 5:10 says, "They hate him that rebukes at the gate and they abhor him that speaketh uprightly."

The enemy hates and abhors anyone who stands in a place of authority and proclaims the truths of God's Word. Interestingly enough, outside the gate is where criminals that had been condemned to death were punished. Let us look at some examples in scripture of what took place at the gates.

Genesis 19:1 (King James Version)

> "¹ And there came two angels to Sodom at even; and Lot sat in the gate of Sodom: and Lot seeing them rose up to meet them; and he bowed himself with his face toward the ground."

We see here that when the angels arrived in Sodom, Lot was sitting at the gate. From all that we have thus learned about the gates, no doubt Lot was some type of political figure at the gate attempting to sway the people of Sodom from their sins and turn their hearts toward God. The Jamieson-Fausset-Brown Bible Commentary said the following concerning Lot:

"Lot sat in the gate of Sodom. In Eastern cities, it is the market, the seat of justice, of social intercourse and amusement, especially a favorite lounge in the evenings, the arched roof affording a pleasant shade."

According to this commentary, <u>Lot was sitting at an East gate</u> and <u>East</u> represents the judgment or correction of God. Today, this is a picture of the corruption that is taking place in our marketplaces, our judicial systems and in the entertainment industry. Lot was trying to no avail to bring about changes in these areas of society; trying to cause those at this East Gate or position of authority to walk upright before God. We all know the rest of the story. God does not look kindly on rebellion as we see below:

Deuteronomy 21:18-20 (King James Version)

"[18] If a man have a stubborn and rebellious son, which will not obey the voice of his father, or the voice of his mother, and that, when they have chastened him, will not hearken unto them:

[19] Then shall his father and his mother lay hold on him, and bring him out unto the elders of his city, and unto the gate of his place;

²⁰ And they shall say unto the elders of his city, This our son is stubborn and rebellious, he will not obey our voice; he is a glutton, and a drunkard.

²¹ And <u>all the men of his city shall stone him with stones, that he die</u>: **so shalt thou put evil away from among you; and all Israel shall hear, and fear."**

Here in Deuteronomy 21:18-20, we find that when parents have as we say in our lingo "hardheaded" children, the children were taken to the gate where the elders were and judged and then stoned to death. Listen, they were serious at the gate and they were not letting anyone or anything corrupt inside the gates; not even children!

Isaiah 29:21 (King James Version)

"²¹ That make a man an offender for a word, and lay a snare for him that reproveth in the gate, and turn aside the just for a thing of nought."

In Isaiah 29:21, there is also a reference to gate as follows, "Him that reproveth in the gate." This scripture reference is talking about the prophets and ministers of God because in those days, people assembled at the gate not only for civil matters but for spiritual matters as well. Therefore, the prophets would sometimes deliver their prophecies at the gate.

There are so many other scriptural references to gates and I advise you to do a study on them for yourself but know that in the Old Testament times, everything that was happening was happening at the gates.

Gates are both naturally and spiritually entry points that have to be strengthened in order to keep the enemy out, to keep the people safe, and to keep our possessions from being plundered. Therefore, the warfare will always be at the gate which is the entry point or the place of authority. The enemy always wants to dethrone the righteous who are at the gates.

Proverbs 29:2 (King James Version)

> "² When the righteous are in authority,
> the people rejoice: but when the wicked
> beareth rule, the people mourn."

Some natural gateways are what we call ports of entry. Dictionary.com defines ports of entry as any place where persons and merchandise are allowed to pass, by water or land, into and out of a country and where customs officers are stationed to inspect or appraise imported goods. The key in this definition is "**are allowed to pass.**" Unless someone in authority gives access at this particular place of entry, it cannot be accessed. In other words, unless it is done illegally, no one can gain access without authorization.

We read in the papers and hear on the news about the wars that take place over various borders. There are major power struggles taking place everyday all over the world because whoever is in authority determines who has access at the gate. The world gives us a clear depiction of what is also taking place in the spiritual realm as well.

The Three Levels of Gates

Within the body of Christ, we as **intercessors** are called to defend three different levels of gates. The first gate is our local church, the second gate consists of our city/region and the third gate is the nations. As an intercessor, you are without any doubt called to defend the gates of your local assembly, but you may or may not be called to defend your city/region and the nations. If you are called to these areas, you will know and your leaders will know as well.

Gate 1
The Local Church

Within the local church, there are several gates that the enemy is attempting to penetrate. His access to these areas would bring great devastation to our local houses. I cannot touch on all of them, but there is one that I know merits our discussion. This gate is the Gate of Praise.

Isaiah 60:18 (King James Version)

"[18] Violence shall no more be heard in thy land, wasting nor destruction within

thy borders; but thou shalt call thy walls
Salvation, and <u>thy gates Praise</u>."

Satan attempts to attack and infiltrate the Praise and
Worship of every local house. He attacks those who
help to usher in the presence of God such as the Praise
and Worship leaders, minstrels and psalmist. If the
Praise and Worship of a house is hindered, then, there
are several areas that will be affected. But before we
jump into what these areas are, let us look at some
reasons that this particular gate is important.

First, Praise and Worship is how we come into
God's presence (Psalm 100:4); second, God inhabits
the praise of His people (Psalm 22:3); thirdly, Praise
and Worship is pleasing to God (Psalm 69: 30-31)
and lastly, God requires our praise and worship as a
sacrifice to Him (Hebrews 13:5).

There are several areas that can be hindered when
there is no pure flow of Praise and Worship in the
house. The most important two of these areas are
<u>healing and deliverance</u>. Praise and Worship creates
an atmosphere that is conducive for healing and
deliverance to flow. Of course, the enemy does not
want to see people healed and delivered so, this is a
gate that he wants access to in order to show that he
can shut it down. **Intercessors,** we must defend this
gate in our local houses.

Psalm 127:5 says that we are to "speak with the
enemies in the gate." That word *speak* is the Hebrew
word "**DABAR**" and it means to command, to subdue
or to warn. **Intercessors,** we have to subdue and

command the devil at the praise gate, we are to let him know that the gates of hell will not prevail, and that our minstrels, psalmist and leaders of Praise and Worship will usher in the presence of God like never before. We cannot just let the enemy come in and disrupt the flow of our Praise and Worship.

Remember Praise and Worship is just the gate I used as an example, but there are many more gates in the local church that need defending and our leaders will strategically place us and guide us in defending these places of authority.

Gate 2
City/Region

The second gate is your <u>city/region</u>. Your local church may be a "Gateway Church" or an "Apostolic House" set in your city/region to impact that area for the glory of God. I have been a part of ministries that were Gateway Churches. These are ministries in a city/region that God has raised up to impact that area. What does that word **impact** mean? It means the striking of one thing against another; forceful contact; collision: influence; effect to drive or press closely or firmly into something; pack in; alter. What a powerful definition.

Can you see why God is raising up **intercessors** to defend this gate? Let us break this thing down. The first meaning given is the striking of one thing against another. <u>Well, when the church impacts a city/region; it is literally the Kingdom of light striking against the kingdom of darkness</u>. The second and third definitions

read forceful contact and collision and this lines up with the word! The Lord Jesus told us about this in the following scripture:
Matthew 11:12 (King James Version)

> "[12] And from the days of John the Baptist until now the kingdom of heaven suffereth violence, and the violent take it by force."

When you are a church called to impact an area, some things just have to be taken by force and there will be a colliding of light and darkness but know this, light always prevails! Hallelujah!

One of the other definitions that I like is <u>alter</u>! I was in a conference and one of the ministers made a statement something to the effect that history belongs to the intercessor. Listen **intercessors,** with our prophetic prayers and intercession, we can aide our local churches in altering the history of our city/region for the Glory of God!!!

Come on **intercessors**, defend the gate to your city/region and watch the very course of history concerning your city/region change. Watch gangbangers become "Glory Carriers," and watch prostitutes become "Preaching Women." Oh my God, the possibilities are endless. Are you fired up yet?

Gate 3
The Nations

The third gate is the <u>gate to the nations</u>. You have to be a part of a strong Apostolic and Prophetic house to operate at this level of defending the gates. These defenders are usually Apostles, Prophets, Prophetic Teachers, and seasoned Prophetic Intercessors.

In Matthew 28:18-20, Jesus told the eleven disciples to go and make disciples or followers of Christ of all nations. That word **nations** is the Greek word **"Ethnos"** and it speaks of a tribe, nation or people group.

The Great Commission

The Lord Jesus gave us the great Commission to go into all nations to make disciples for Him as recorded by the Apostle Matthew:

Matthew 28:16-20 (New International Version)

"[16] Then the eleven disciples went to Galilee, to the mountain where Jesus had told them to go.

[17] When they saw him, they worshiped him; but some doubted.

[18] Then Jesus came to them and said, "All authority in heaven and on earth has been given to me.

[19] Therefore go and make disciples of all nations, baptizing them in the name of the Father and of the Son and of the Holy Spirit,

[20] and teaching them to obey everything I have commanded you. And surely I

am with you always, to the very end of
the age."

This text is Apostolic because Jesus is the Great Apostle
and he is sending us out to make followers of Christ
not only amongst of the Jews, but past Judea and to
all ethnos. We have to make sure that we are sent
when it comes to defending the nations. This is high
level warfare and the enemy will resist and struggle
with you at these gates. These levels of demons do not
yield quietly, but as an intercessor called to defend the
nations, you can rebuke the enemy at the gate. It is all
about knowing our sphere of authority.

Amos 5:10 (King James Version)

"[10] They hate him that rebuketh in the
gate, and they abhor him that speaketh
uprightly."

Conclusion

Intercessors, we play a vital part in maintaining the health and wealth of the local church and the body of Christ at large. God called, chosen men and women of God and He commissioned them to make disciples of nations. Along with that commission, He gave them instructions on how to go about doing it. The enemy knows his fate and that his time is short so, he is doing everything he can to oppose the Kingdom of God and those commissioned to its advancement.

God has set us in the body to aide our leaders by defending them, defending the house, defending the vision and defending the gates. He has "graced" you and me to do it. Through our prophetic prayers and intercession, our Praise and Worship and our studying the word to identify the enemy, we can then decree and declare God's Word over what we see so that we can make a difference. We are already making a difference!

Therefore, I encourage you to stay on the wall and refuse to come down; knowing that the greater one is on the inside of you and that if God is for you, He is more than all the devils in hell that are against you. You are an elite generation of warriors that God is raising up to assault the kingdom of darkness. I charge you to take ownership and decree and declare into the atmosphere right now that you will secure and fortify your local house through the weapon of intercession! May God bless you.

— **Dr. Ceretta Smith**

About the Author

Dr. **Ceretta Smith** is native of Fayetteville, NC and a U.S. Army Veteran. She currently resides in Augusta, GA with her husband, Retired SFC Sterling V. Smith and their three sons. She holds a Bachelor Degree in Biblical Studies and Theology, a Masters Degree in Guidance and Counseling and an Honorary Doctorate of Divinity. She is the author of *The Black Sheep a Leader in These Latter Days*, **The Gift Of The Teacher: A Practical Biblical Guide,** and a recording artist. Dr. Smith has a strong teaching anointing and hopes this book will empower all the prayer warriors that read it. She attends church at First Baptist Church Keysville, Inc., in Hephzibah, Georgia.

Other Books by the Author

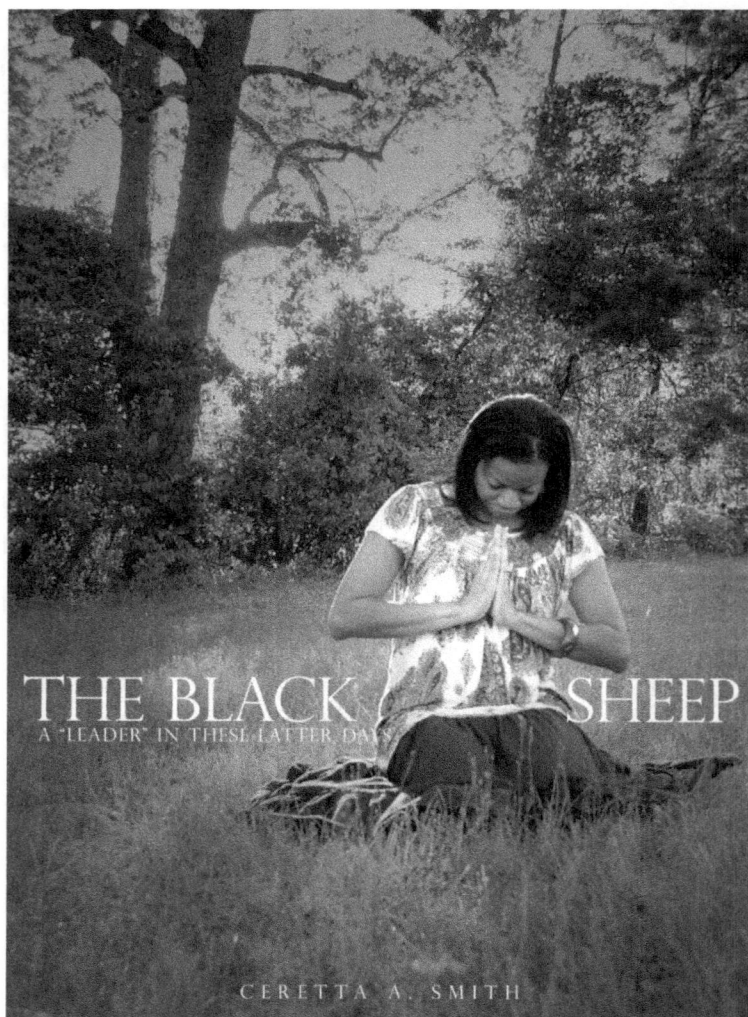

THE BLACK SHEEP
A "LEADER" IN THESE LATTER DAYS

CERETTA A. SMITH

The Black Sheep: A Leader in These Latter Days

You've heard the old phrase, "Sticks and stones may break my bones, but words will never hurt me." This expression rings true only partially for you and I just like millions of other people. There are few among us who have managed to escape the pain inflicted by hateful words. We might pretend to be healthy and whole, but the words fester in our hearts and minds, sometimes causing a lifetime of agony.

If you are strong enough to admit that you have allowed your self-esteem to be bruised by slander, this book is for you. When you break a bone, you don't pretend that it isn't broken or that it doesn't hurt. No, you seek medical attention so that the healing process can begin. In some cases, the broken bone leaves a scar as a reminder of the place of pain, but the scar itself represents healing. There is no shame or weakness in admitting that words can hurt just as much as physical injury, oftentimes more. Words can pierce deep into the soul, leaving wounds that will bleed for a lifetime unless we remedy them.

Three words- "The Black Sheep"- haunted me for many, many years. As a result of the process revealed in this book, I am no longer a victim to this taunt. My life has been transformed by admitting the hurt, banishing the lies, and embracing the truth. You too will be released from the stigma of these words by the advice in these pages. When you are finished with this book, you'll remember that catchy phrase much differently; "Sticks and stones may break my bones, but I will never allow the pain of negative words to hold me captive."

Operating in The Gift Of The Teacher
A Practical Biblical Guide

To:Teachers

Dr. Ceretta A. Smith

Operating in the Gift of the Teacher: A Practical Biblical Guide

This book is about re-introducing the body of Christ to the <u>teaching gift</u> because great emphasis has been placed on the other five fold ministry gifts but that of the **Teacher** seems to have been overlooked and not developed in those who have the gift. It outlines how to develop the gift of the teacher and it contains teaching techniques that will help the reader to attain to a higher level of excellence and challenge those who have been complacent with the gift. It is a must read for all those who have been called to teach.

Bibliography

Brown, Driver, Briggs and Gesenius. "Hebrew Lexicon entry for `etsah". "*The Old Testament Hebrew Lexicon*". <http://www.studylight.org/lex/heb/view. cgi?number=6098>.

Brown, Driver, Briggs and Gesenius. "Hebrew Lexicon entry for Shamar". "*The Old Testament Hebrew Lexicon*". <http://www.studylight.org/lex/heb/view. cgi?number=8104>.

Gossip. (n.d.). Collins English Dictionary - Complete & Unabridged 10th Edition. Retrieved September 22, 2012, from *Dictionary.com* website: <http://dictionary. reference.com/browse/gossip>.

Meir, Tamar. "Orpah: Midrash and Aggadah." *Jewish Women: A Comprehensive Historical Encyclopedia*. 1 March 2009. Jewish Women's Archive. (Viewed on September 22, 2012) <http://jwa.org/encyclopedia/ article/orpah-midrash-and-aggadah>.

Thayer and Smith. "Greek Lexicon entry for Ekklesia". "*The New Testament Greek Lexicon*". <http://www.studylight.org/lex/grk/view. cgi?number=1577>.

Thayer and Smith. "Greek Lexicon entry for Oikos". "The New Testament Greek Lexicon". <http://www.studylight.org/lex/grk/view. cgi?number=3624>.

TO HIS GLORY PUBLISHING COMPANY, INC.

463 Dogwood Dr. Lilburn, GA. 30047, U.S.A (770)458-7947

Order Form for Bookstores in the USA

Order Date: _____

Order Placed By: _____   By Fax: _____

Address: _____

_____

City _____ ST/ZIP _____

Phone #: _____

Email: _____

Purchase Order#: _____

Return Policy: Within 1 year but not before 90 Days.

Price	**Quantity**	**List Price**
Shipping Method:		
Media:		
UPS:		
FedEx:		
Other (Please Secify):		
Total Price:	**Total Quantity:**	**List Price**

Ship To Address: **Bill to Address:**

To His Glory Publishing

Let Us Publish Your Book

To His Glory Publishing Company will publish your book at the least expensive cost. We pay one of the highest royalties in the industry – 40%! We print on demand and place your book on the major online bookstores such a Amazon.com, Barnesandnoble.com, Bookamillion.com, etc.

www.ingramcontent.com/pod-product-compliance
Lightning Source LLC
LaVergne TN
LVHW021541080426
835509LV00019B/2768